THE GOLDEN YEARS OF RAILROADING

THE NEW HAVEN RAILROAD ALONG THE SHORE LINE

The thoroughfare from New York City to Boston

MARTIN J. McGUIRK

KALMBACH BOOKS

© 1999 Kalmbach Publishing Co. All rights reserved. This book may not be reproduced in part or in whole without written permission of the publisher, except in the case of brief quotations used in reviews. Published by Kalmbach Publishing Co., 21027 Crossroads Circle, Waukesha, WI 53187.

Printed in the United States of America

98 99 00 01 02 03 04 05 06 07   10 9 8 7 6 5 4 3 2 1

For more information, visit our website at http://www.kalmbach.com

On the Cover: Nothing says "New Haven" like heavy electric locomotives. Noted railroad photographer Jim Shaughnessy captured EP-5 no. 379, looking freshly washed, as it sat in New Haven awaiting its next assignment to New York City. The EP-5 wears the McGinnis colors of red, white, and black, while barely visible to the left is an older electric, still wearing classic green with gold pinstripes.

Book and cover design: Kristi Ludwig

Publisher's Cataloging-in-Publication
(Provided by Quality Books, Inc.)

McGuirk, Martin.
  The New Haven Railroad along the Shore Line : the thoroughfare from New York City to Boston / Martin McGuirk.
  — 1st ed.
  p. cm. — (Golden Years of Railroading)
  Includes index.
  ISBN: 0-89024-344-1

  1. New Haven Railroad—History. 2. Railroads—New England.
3. Railroads—New York (State) I. Title. II. Series.

TS25.N4M3 1998   385´.0974
                                                    QBI98-577

Contents

A brief history of the New York, New Haven & Hartford 5

Railroading in Gotham 13

The West End 29

    EP-3: Forerunner to a legend 40

    FL9: True diesel electric 46

The New Haven in its hometown 49

Maybrook Line: Freight artery 65

The Shore Line 83

The New Haven in Boston 101

The New Haven today 125

Acknowledgments 126

Index of photographs 127

From 1941 through early 1952, mainline steam, diesel, and electric road power coexisted on the New York, New Haven & Hartford. Here we see an example of each type of power. From left to right: An Alco DL109, a Baldwin I-5 class streamlined Hudson, and an EP-4 electric "motor" lined up in New Haven. NYNH&H photo, January 1950

A brief history of the New York, New Haven & Hartford

The New York, New Haven & Hartford of the 1940s and '50s was not the largest railroad in the United States, but it was one of the most varied. It was unusual for several reasons. In a nation where the majority of trains were pulled by steam and, later, diesel locomotives, the New Haven experienced great success using heavy electric locomotives on some of its busiest routes. While the majority of railroads made the lion's share of revenue hauling freight, the New Haven derived a large percentage of its revenue from passenger receipts. In mileage, the New Haven was the 39th largest American railroad. But it was third in passenger miles. This statistic is even more amazing when you consider how short the New Haven main line was. Essentially, the railroad connected New York City with Boston. Except for short incursions into New York, all of the New Haven was contained within the states of Connecticut, Massachusetts, and Rhode Island.

An amazing characteristic of the New Haven was the density of the routes it maintained within such a small geographic area.

Owing to the nature of the industries in the area the railroad served, the New Haven was handicapped throughout its history by unbalanced freight traffic. Most of the freight cars the railroad hauled into New England were loads of raw materials. Most outbound traffic was overwhelmingly empty cars, cars that generated no revenue for the New Haven. Good thing the passenger traffic was there to make up the difference!

Passenger service ran the gamut from Budd Rail Diesel Cars on branch lines to commuter trains operating between Boston and New York City and their suburbs, up to a series of name trains that were second to none: the *Pilgrim, Bankers,* the *Yankee Clipper,* and the *Merchants Limited* were all considered the way to travel for the better part of three decades.

Yes, the New Haven ran the varnish in style over the years, and when the passengers abandoned the trains in favor of a quick and easy drive along Interstate 95 between New York City and Boston, the railroad felt the loss, and felt it hard.

Like most railroad companies that matured in the late nineteenth century, the New Haven was really the creation of financiers and bankers who combined smaller, unprofitable systems into one large money-making concern. Starting as the New York & New Haven, the railroad brought hundreds of smaller companies into its fold by the early years of this century. Rather than compete for traffic with parallel routes, the New Haven simply bought them up until it controlled virtually every mile of track in Connecticut, Rhode Island, and much of Massachusetts.

This policy of expansion through acquisition would eventually be a key contributor to the railroad's downfall—those lines that were acquired at great cost would never generate enough revenue to be remotely profitable.

The four principal companies that eventually became the New Haven of the 1940s and '50s were the New York & New Haven, the Old Colony, the New York & New England, and the Central New England. Of these, the NY&NH, referred to as the New Haven, was the most significant.

The focus of this book is on the New Haven of the 1940s and '50s. But in order to understand how the railroad came to be we must look at the background of these four key components.

Early history

Railroading in Connecticut got off to a comparatively late start, primarily because of the well-developed water and road transportation along the state's many rivers. The earliest routes aimed inland. The first line to operate what would become New Haven trackage was Hartford & New Haven, chartered in 1833. By 1839 this line was operating between its namesake cities and by 1844 the line extended north to Springfield, Mass. That same year the New York & New Haven Railroad was chartered in Connecticut. The New York & Harlem opposed the chartering of the line into New York state until it was agreed that the NY&NH would use the NY&H's tracks into New York City. The line was completed in 1848; the biggest construction challenge was bridging a large number of waterways and estuaries, since the line paralleled Long Island Sound.

In 1848 the first portion of the New Haven & Northhampton opened between New Haven and Plainville, Conn., following a route formed by an old canal. This route, nicknamed the Canal Line, was leased by the NY&NH to compete directly with the H&NH.

It was also in 1848 that the New Haven & New London opened between New Haven and Stonington, Conn., with ferries transferring whole trains across the Connecticut and Thames Rivers. By 1870 this route, reorganized as the Shore Line Railway, was leased to the New York & New Haven. The river interests lost their fight to keep the railroad from bridging the rivers, and the Connecticut was bridged in 1870. The Thames remained unbridged until 1889.

Consolidation and more expansion

The New York, New Haven & Hartford Railroad came into existence on August 6, 1872, with the consolidation of the NY&NH and the H&NH. The newly created company had close affiliations with the Housatonic and Naugatuck Railroads and reacquired control of the Canal Line in 1881. (The original NY&NH lease expired in 1869.) In 1882 the NYNH&H leased the New Haven to Willimantic Air Line and bought the Hartford & Connecticut Valley between Hartford and Saybrook. In 1892 the New York, Providence & Boston was leased. And in 1893 the NYNH&H

completed its all-rail route between Boston and New York City with the acquisition of the Old Colony, which had a network of lines around Boston. In fact, the Old Colony was about the same size as the New York, New Haven, & Hartford—effectively doubling the size of the railroad.

If the New Haven had any real competition in the 1800s it was the New York & New England. At its zenith, the NY&NE stretched from Boston and Providence through Hartford to the Hudson River in New York state. Branches to Springfield and Worcester, both in Massachusetts, stretched north from the main line. The NY&NE can trace its ancestry back to 1833, when the Manchester Railroad was chartered to build east from Hartford, through the thriving mill town of Manchester, to Bolton, Mass. A lack of funding kept the Manchester Railroad as a paper project until a group of Rhode Island businessmen, bent on building a railroad to serve the growing mill towns in Rhode Island and the eastern part of Connecticut, got into the act. The project quickly blossomed into a line connecting Providence, R. I., with the Hudson River at Fishkill Landing (later Beacon) in New York. This time the project got past the paper stage, and the renamed Hartford, Providence & Fishkill opened for service between Providence and Waterbury, Conn., in 1855.

In 1849 a small railroad, the Norfolk County, opened between Boston and through Walpole to Blackstone, Mass. At the same time, several smaller lines, chief among them the Boston & New York, assembled a route, the Boston & Albany, through Brookline, Mass., and Woonsocket, R. I. The Norfolk County, reorganized and renamed the Hartford & Erie, combined with B&NY and HP&F in 1864 to create a route between Boston and Mechanicville, Conn.

The Boston, Hartford & Erie entered bankruptcy in 1870, emerging as the New York & New England. By 1881 the NY&NE reached the Hudson River. By this point the New Haven, which had even operated the joint New England Limited with the NY&NE, began to look upon its northern neighbor as a serious threat. Every few miles the NY&NE crossed a railroad that offered a connection to New York City, but virtually all those connections depended on the New Haven. One by one, the NH choked off those connections, cutting off the NY&NE while the New Haven system expanded.

The New Haven took over the Housatonic Railroad, which operated a joint train/ferryboat service into New York City with the NY&NE via the Housatonic's steamboat pier in Oyster Bay, just south of Norwalk. The New York Central even got into the act when it took over, at the New Haven's request, the New York & Northern, another potential NY&NE connection.

By 1893 the NY&NE, its friendly connections acquired by the rapidly expanding New Haven, was cut off. The company filed for bankruptcy and was acquired by the NH in 1898.

The age of robber barons

By the turn of the century the New Haven of the 1950s was essentially in place, although significant changes would take place along portions of the line. More important, the New Haven came under the scrutiny of James P. Morgan. Morgan, a banker who was born in Hartford, took a fair amount of interest in his hometown railroad, reputedly insisting on calling it the "Hartford."

By the late 1890s Charles Mellen, one of J. P. Morgan's protégés, was determined to control all the railroads in New England. He bought all the street and interurban railroads in the New Haven's territory as well as the Boston & Maine and Maine Central railroads. Jointly with the New York Central he purchased the Rutland. He also acquired the New York, Ontario & Western. Mellen also started constructing the New York, Westchester & Boston, an ill-conceived interurban line that paralleled already existing New Haven track between New York City and Port Chester, with a branch line to White Plains.

While the New Haven had early visions of expansion into northern New England, an agreement with the Boston & Maine was honored. The B&M would not seek to expand south of the Boston & Albany, and the New Haven wouldn't go north. With the exception of some routes already in place in western Massachusetts, the NH honored this agreement.

The New Haven emerged from its years of Mellen's control a thoroughly modern railroad. But the cost of electrifying the main line between New York City and New Haven and constructing the New York Connecting Railroad and Hell Gate Bridge would have certainly resulted in bankruptcy if the New Haven, like virtually every other railroad, had not come under the control of the United States Railroad Administration during World War I. With the return of peace, the USRA relinquished control and the New Haven soldiered on.

By the late 1920s the Pennsylvania Railroad acquired control of nearly one-fourth of the New Haven's outstanding stock. Both the Pennsylvania and the New Haven acquired Boston & Maine stock, effectively resuming the New Haven's financial control of that line. The Great Depression had the same effect on the New Haven that it had on many other businesses, and the line filed for bankruptcy in October 1935.

Reorganization and the war years

The bankrupt line set about to reorganize into a leaner, more efficient railroad. Steamship lines owned by the railroad were liquidated. Unprofitable branch lines, including Mellen's pet project New York, Westchester & Boston, were also eliminated. In 1938 the New Haven, by now aware of the significant threat presented to freight traffic by its short main line, instituted piggyback service.

During the Second World War, the New Haven, this time retaining independent control, was put to the test. It passed with flying colors. The numbers don't really tell the story. In 1938 the line carried 16 million tons of freight. By 1941 that number had risen to 27 million, and by 1943 to a staggering 38 million tons—all the while moving record numbers of civilian and military passengers.

Mismanagement and the inevitable decline

If the war years had been the New Haven's finest hour, the 1950s were a decade marked by bad decision-making and downright incompetence on the part of the railroad's upper-level management.

The reorganization ended on September 17, 1947. Frederic C. Dulmaine and others, including a man named Patrick McGinnis, took control of the New Haven. The experienced executives who had seen the railroad through the reorganization, Depression, and record traffic of the war years were pushed aside. In 1951 Frederic Dulmaine died and control passed to his son, Frederic, Jr. He set out to restore morale and improve the physical condition of the railroad, still suffering from the heavy use of the war years and the deferred maintenance of the Depression.

Despite Dulmaine's best intentions, he lost control of the railroad to Patrick McGinnis after a 1953 proxy fight. Obsessed with the bottom line, McGinnis slashed maintenance and ordered expensive, experimental lightweight trains to replace the almost-new conventional passenger trains in Boston–New York service. McGinnis's most visible effect on the railroad was the striking red, white, and black color scheme applied to locomotives, a significant change from the sedate but dignified hunter green and yellow of the 1940s.

The McGinnis era was the beginning of the end for the New Haven. Commuters, who made up a considerable percentage of the railroad's riders, were a money-losing necessity. The railroad imposed parking charges at lots in suburban stations, driving commuters away by the thousands. Not all his underlings agreed with his policies, and many directors resigned from the board. McGinnis left the New Haven in 1956 to take control of the Boston & Maine. Auditors soon shocked stockholders by revealing that the near-record earnings between 1953 and '56 had been, in actuality, less than half of the amount McGinnis reported.

The effect of Patrick McGinnis's short reign on the New Haven outlasted his stint in the director's chair. George Alpert took control of the railroad just as the lightweight trains McGinnis had purchased arrived. These trains, heralded as the future of train travel, were public-relations and mechanical disasters. Perhaps it was an omen when one of these trains caught fire during an inaugural run with members of the press on board and derailed later the same day. Piggyback traffic, which the New Haven had initiated before the war, disappeared as truckers and railroads west of New York found they could achieve faster deliveries to New England destinations by unloading the trailers from flats in New York and using the newly completed Connecticut Turnpike, which paralleled the New Haven's main line between Boston and New York.

The poor decision-making continued. In 1956, as one of McGinnis's last acts, the New Haven ordered 60 FL9s from EMD. These unique locomotives were intended to eliminate all electrics from service on the railroad; they could run on straight diesel power above ground or, using a pickup shoe, on the NYC's 650-volt DC third rail into New York. Money-short New Haven ordered these units a mere 12 months after taking delivery of ten brand-new EP-5 passenger electric locomotives and more than 100 M.U. cars, all of which were designed to operate using the very catenary system the FL9s were designed to replace.

An influx of loans from the Interstate Commerce Commission kept the New Haven solvent until 1961. By July of that year the New Haven was back into reorganization, petitioning for inclusion in the planned New York Central–Pennsylvania Railroad merger. The two larger railroads agreed, with the stipulation that the New Haven be free of passenger service. This request was denied by the ICC. On December 2, 1968, the ICC ruled that the Penn Central would take control of the New Haven by the beginning of 1969. On December 31, 1968, Penn Central purchased all the New Haven's properties and the New Haven, as a legal entity, ceased to exist.

The New Haven's legacy

Financial maneuverings and poor management aside, the New Haven's legacy, as viewed by passengers, employees, and railfans, was heavy-duty railroading at its best. Here was a railroad that railroaded to a level rarely, if ever equaled on this continent.

The sheer number of passenger trains operated per day into New York City and Boston staggers the imagination of today's railfans, who are happy to see one, or maybe two, trains on a day's outing. There were the limited trains, the express and mail trains, the commuter runs, and the local accommodation trains. Intermixed before, after, and during them were long freights. All of these were headed by a roster of steam, diesel, and electric locomotives as unique and varied as the railroad they served.

While it had track reaching into every hamlet and township in southern New England, the core of the New Haven was always the corridor between New York City and Boston. In New York City, the New York Central had Grand Central Terminal and the Pennsylvania controlled mighty Penn Station, but the New Haven served both of them. The New Haven's two New York City routes converged at New Rochelle, and from there four-track main line headed east under wire to New Haven. Most trains had locomotives changed here. Trains bound for New York had their diesel or steam power replaced by electrics. The reverse happened to trains arriving from New York.

In New Haven the railroad split, with one line heading north to Hartford and Springfield, Mass. The second line was the Shore Line route east along the Connecticut coast to Boston.

The principal overland freight route for traffic heading into and out of New England was the line from Maybrook, N. Y., which headed through the Connecticut countryside before joining the four-track main route just outside Milford, Conn. The New Haven also maintained an active level of freight interchange in New York City with the Pennsylvania Railroad via carfloats that operated across New York harbor.

This book is a photographic journey along the railroad's New York–Boston core as it was in the 1940s and '50s. Our journey starts with a look at operations in New York City. Then we'll follow the railroad east through Connecticut until we reach the end of the line in Massachusetts.

The New Haven operated into Grand Central on trackage rights. One of the New Haven's unique FL9s shares a platform with one of New York Central's (ex–Cleveland Union Terminal) electrics in Grand Central Terminal. Underground, the FL9 picks up power from the NYC's 650-volt DC third rail. Above ground, the FL9 runs using its onboard EMD power plant. Photo by Jim Shaughnessy

Railroading in Gotham

The New York state legislature changed the look of railroads in New York City forever on May 7, 1903, when it passed an ordinance forbidding steam locomotives from entering Grand Central and its approaches after July 1, 1908. The law was the direct result of an accident in one of the city's many railroad tunnels. Steam locomotive smoke had caused the poor visibility that led to the accident. The new law sent the railroads that served New York scrambling to find other options for powering trains. Diesel locomotives were still decades away, and their fumes would have been just as deadly as the steamers. The only practical solution, then and now, was electric power.

AC or DC?

The New York Central & Hudson River Railroad, which owned the trackage affected by the new legislation, quickly signed contracts for locomotives and substations to convert its line to 650-volt direct current provided by a third rail located at ground level alongside the track. Installation of this system was completed in July 1907.

It was assumed that the NH would simply institute a steam-to-electric locomotive change point near its connection with the New York Central at Woodlawn Junction, located just inside the city boundary in the Bronx.

But the New Haven had experience with DC electrification on a number of branch and trolley lines, and its engineers knew that DC power, which was excellent for light traction lines, demonstrated significant voltage drop when used for heavy railroad electrification. A line of any length required frequent substations to maintain the enormous current required to move trains with such low voltage.

Enter Westinghouse Electric and Manufacturing Co. They proposed an 11,000-volt alternating current system for the New Haven. The railroad's engineering staff looked at the big picture. It was felt that electrifying the railroad wouldn't be cost-effective unless the wires went east to Stamford, Connecticut, the end of the suburban district. But low-voltage DC was inadequate for such long distances. At the same time, while DC power was proven and reliable, AC power, especially in the scale needed by the NH, was relatively untested.

In 1905 the New Haven surprised many industry experts when it announced plans to go with the 11,000-volt single-phase alternating current proposal from Westinghouse. Forty-one electric locomotives, and all the generating and transmission equipment needed, were ordered from Westinghouse.

This decision had a profound effect upon New Haven locomotive design, since the NH had to use NYC motive power over the DC section into Grand Central, purchase DC locomotives and institute a locomotive change point at Woodlawn, or come up with a way for locomotives to work on either AC or DC. The first two choices weren't practical options, so the only solution was a dual-voltage locomotive.

Not only did the locomotives have to pick up power from an overhead wire, located up to 22 feet above the rails, they also had to be able to run on lower-voltage DC power delivered from a third rail on either side of the track or from overhead rails just above roof level in the complex Grand Central trackwork. And they had to perform these changes at speed. They eventually succeeded, and the same system is still used by modern commuter trains heading into New York City today. The New Haven's electrification was considered a complete success, and was eventually extended as far as New Haven.

Freight service in New York City

The lion's share of New Haven trains into New York City carried passengers, but the railroad also operated a considerable freight business in and around New York. The largest freight classification yard in the city was Oak Point, located in the Bronx. With a total of 35 miles of track under wire, Oak Point was at one time the largest electrified railroad yard in the world.

Ironically, the most interesting motive power in Oak Point wasn't locomotives, but boats. The New Haven, like all railroads in New York City, relied on an extensive navy of tugboats (on the New Haven they were called transfers) and carfloats to transfer freight to and from Manhattan Island and across the Hudson and East Rivers to connections with railroads on the Jersey side.

From Oak Point, cars destined for interchange with the Lehigh Valley and Central of New Jersey were loaded onto car floats for the 12-mile (1½-hour) journey to the piers at Jersey City. Prior to the opening of the Hell Gate Bridge, cars destined for the Pennsy would travel 15 miles to the connection to the PRR docks in Greenville, N. J. With the opening of the bridge, freight passed over the bridge all the way to Bay Ridge, traversed the Long Island Railroad for a short distance, and was then loaded on a car float for a quick trip across Upper New York Bay to Greenville.

By the 1950s the New Haven's fleet numbered nine tugs, the newest of which was more than four decades old. The New Haven ordered eight new diesel-powered tugs, including the *Cordelia* and the *Bumble Bee*, which were soon renamed *Transfer 23* and *24*, respectively.

The McGinnis management canceled the orders for the remaining six boats. Instead, three additional tugs were leased from the Dalzell Harbor Corp. in 1957. The five diesel tugs handled the New Haven's floating requirements until the Penn Central merger in 1969.

Hell Gate Bridge and access to Penn Station

For almost the first two decades of this century a direct rail connection between the busy New Haven Boston–New York rail route and the Pennsylvania Washington, D. C.–New York route was impossible. Even more amazing, the two railroads were separated by less than six miles. But that six miles included the East River.

The solution was a bridge across the Hell Gate, a narrow channel on the East River, that would link Long Island and the mainland.

The idea of a bridge across Hell Gate dated back to the formation of the New York Connecting Railroad in 1892. The railroad was to proceed from Westchester County to Brooklyn, following a route almost identical to the one eventually used by the Pennsy. The New York Connecting Railroad lay dormant for a decade, the cost of such a project far outweighing any potential return, until the Pennsy and the New Haven bought the company.

Hell Gate Bridge

Construction of the bridge actually started in 1912. The bridge measures 1,017 feet between the two masonry towers. The topmost point of the arch is 305 feet above mean high water, and the deck of the bridge carries four electrified tracks.

Just as significant as the bridge itself are the extensive approaches that climb a 1.2 percent grade from the connection with the New Haven at Port Morris before crossing Ward's Island on a sharp curve. Between Ward's and Randall Islands is a 400-foot-long four-span deck truss bridge. The final landmark on the New York Connecting Railroad is a double bascule bridge across Bronx Kill.

The first revenue trip by a passenger train over Hell Gate Bridge was made on April 1, 1917.

When first completed, the bridge and its approaches were highly visible parts of the New York skyline. Roadway bridges and the urban development of the areas around the bridge have made it far less prominent today. But the unique and attractive span, with its unmistakable silhouette, is still as striking as the first day it opened.

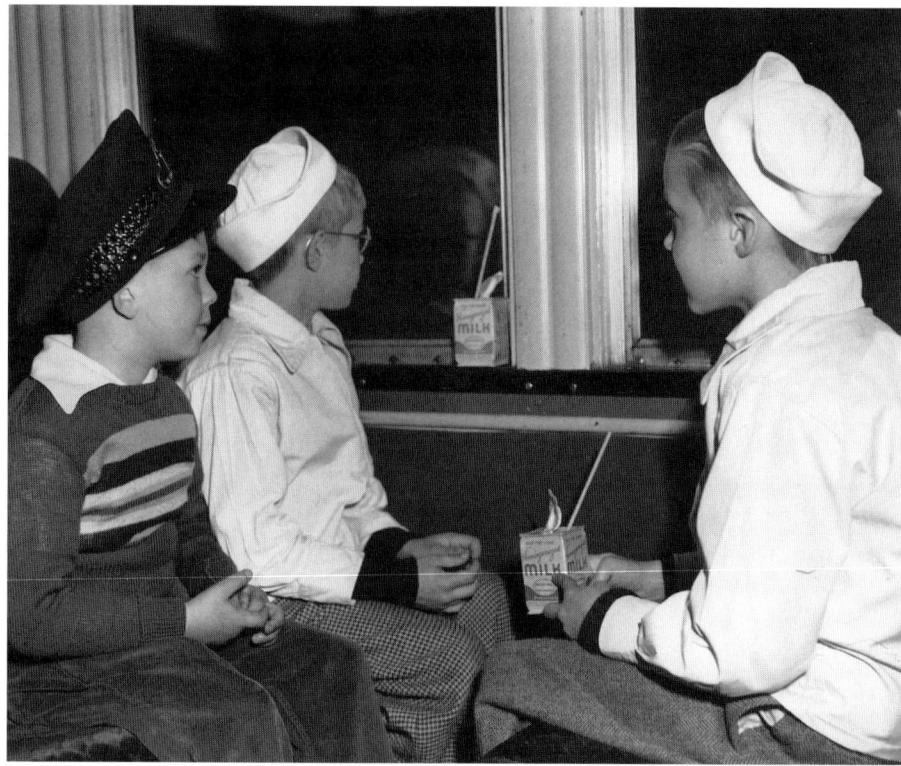

This trio looks very patriotic as they enjoy a beverage on one of the dozens of passenger trains that departed Grand Central daily. NYNH&H photo

The Owl is the most famous of several night trains between New York and Boston, perhaps best remembered for its all-sleeping-car consist. Departure is set for 12:30 a.m., but passengers could start boarding the train as early as 10:00 p.m.—a perfect schedule for catching a Broadway show and then retiring to the sleeping car for a comfortable night's sleep. Photo by Don Wood

This train of westbound M.U. cars is crossing the flyover track at Woodlawn Junction, New York. It has just left the New Haven's rails, and 11,000-volt AC catenary, and is drawing power from the New York Central's 650-volt DC third rail. Those are the tracks of the NYC below, and the train will quickly drop down to meet them for the remainder of the trip into Grand Central. Photo by Frank W. Schlegel, December 24, 1952

Almost-new electric freight motor No. 0155 is hard at work at the point of a wartime freight in Port Chester, New York. The 0155 and its four sisters (0156–0159) were classed as EF-3a. Nearly identical EF-3s 0150–0154 were built by Baldwin-Westinghouse in 1942. The EF-3a's were built by General Electric in 1943. Each of these brutes could haul 5,000 tons, or about 125 carloads. With coastal shipping threatened by German submarine attack, these engines played a critical role in handling war traffic on the Cedar Hill–Oak Point route. May 24, 1943

"Brick canyons" would be an appropriate description for this scene showing EP-4 No. 361 heading a Grand Central–bound passenger train out of the city. New Haven motors were classified by type of service and class number. EP-4 is Electric, Passenger, fourth class of that type assigned by the railroad. Photographer unknown, September 11, 1952

Show posters have always been a part of the scenery on platforms in the New York area. Here one of the 104 Multiple Unit Cars (nicknamed MUTs) glides into New Rochelle, New York. These heavyweight round-roofed cars were built from 1926 to 1931, and many of them outlasted the railroad. To the relief of New York and Connecticut commuters, all are now retired. Photo by Paul J. Dolkos, July 11, 1955

A Grand Central–bound M.U. train passes a mixed five-car eastbound consist headed by EP-5 "Jet" No. 371. Both trains are running on third-rail territory, along the famed Park Avenue viaduct near Harlem. The stainless-steel M.U. cars were quickly nicknamed "Washboards" because their fluted sides resembled that old household device. Photo by David Plowden, December, 1961

The New Haven was always good about running excursion and special trips for railfan groups or local civic organizations. This train of open-end M.U. cars is preparing to leave Grand Central for an excursion to Van Nest Shops, Harlem River, and Hell Gate Bridge. Photo by Kent Cochrane, June 5, 1948

This happy bunch is heading for the Husking Bee in Kent, Connecticut. This annual event, sponsored every October by the Kent Grange, consisted of a barn dance, a barbecue dinner, and other fun and games. The New Haven's annual special train left Grand Central Terminal for Kent, leaving New York around noon and returning around midnight. The train developed a huge following, attracting 485 riders for its 1949 run. Although the train is about to depart Kent, the photo seemed to fit better with the New York section of this book. NYNH&H photo, October 1948

A New York–bound EP-2 has just about completed its crossing of the Harlem River drawbridge. The bridge in this photo is the predecessor of the present-day bridge. New York Central photo

The sheer size of New York harbor required railroads to maintain "navies" to connect the myriad of islands and terminals. With two exceptions (*Cordelia* and *Bumble Bee*), all the New Haven's tugs were named *Transfer* and numbered sequentially. *Transfer No. 14* is lashed between a pair of carfloats as it heads downriver with cars for the Pennsylvania Railroad at Greenville, New Jersey. NYNH&H photo, August 1943

The unmistakable outline of the Hell Gate Bridge looms ahead of a pair of New Haven carfloats, viewed from a New Haven tug. Completed in 1917, the bridge shortened but did not eliminate the carfloat operation between Oak Point, New York, and Greenville, New Jersey. The bridge was a key link between the New Haven and the Pennsylvania Railroad. The New Haven Marine Department is long gone, but Hell Gate is still used today. NYNH&H photo

A quartet of New Haven EF-1 "Jeeps" heads a long freight across the Hell Gate Bridge. The train originated in the Long Island Railroad's Bay Ridge terminal and consists primarily of cars brought via car floats from the Pennsy's Greenville, New Jersey, terminal. The photographers are from a Joint Railfan Trip Committee special. Photo by Alfred F. Tyrrill, June 5, 1948

About the only time M.U. trains used Hell Gate was for railfan specials. This is the same railfan special we saw sitting in Grand Central (page 21), which brought the photographers to the bridge. Here the train climbs the 1.2 percent grade to the bridge. Photo by Kent Cochrane, June 5, 1948

Head-end business looks pretty good as the Boston-bound *William Penn* crosses Hell Gate on a hot summer morning. The McGinnis black, red, and white scheme is unmistakable, even through the road grime on EP-5 No. 371. Photo by Gary Gadziala, July 1961

There is a short stretch of daylighted track between New York's Penn Station and the tunnels leading out of the city. A New Haven EP-5 "Jet," just in from New Haven, sits in the open area west of Penn Station. Photo by Alan M. Schreibman, February, 23, 1959

Classic New Haven: An EP-5, its McGinnis color scheme covered with road grime, heads train No. 181, the *Hell Gate,* through West Haven, Connecticut. Don't let the boxcar fool you—this is a passenger train. Head-end business looks good today. Photo by Bruce Meyer, January 12, 1961

The West End

The four-track line between New Rochelle, New York, and New Haven was the busiest line on the railroad. Almost every New Haven train touched the rails of the West End at one point during its journey over the railroad. The wires were strung over the tracks from New York as far as Stamford, Connecticut, by 1907. Soon afterward, management, pleased with the performance of their electrified main line, extended the wires east as far as New Haven by 1914. For the first mile or so east of Stamford, in the community of Glenbrook, the straight-legged lattice towers that supported the wires, called bridges, gave way to graceful curved arched supports. These were quickly superseded by taper-legged bridges all the way to New Haven. Likewise, the New Haven's unique, and attractive, triangular catenary doesn't extend east of Stamford.

From New York, the tracks crossed the Connecticut state line at Greenwich and proceeded to Stamford, one of the state's largest cities and the east end of the New York suburban district. Just west of Stamford, in the community of Cos Cob, the New Haven maintained a large coal-fired power plant that provided the electricity to feed the 11,000-volt AC power to the wires.

From Stamford, an eight-mile-long branch left the main and headed to New Canaan. Several miles east, in Norwalk, another secondary line swung north to the community of Danbury. This line was under wire until 1961 and saw heavy electric locomotives in both freight and passenger service.

Between Bridgeport and New Haven was one of the most important junction points on the railroad, Devon. This was the place where freights to and from the Maybrook and the Naugatuck lines entered and left the main line for their runs to and from Cedar Hill yard in New Haven. From Devon it was a short jaunt east to New Haven proper.

The West End played host to a variety of steam and diesel locomotives over the years, but these were the intruders, at least until the arrival of the FL9s. The true kings of the West End were heavy electric locomotives—"motors" in New Haven parlance—and they covered all assignments in and out of the city. By the end of the 1950s, the only remaining electrics on the New Haven roster were the ten General Electric ignitron rectifier EP-5s, known as "Jets." Until 1963 the New Haven engaged in the wasteful practice of running fuel-burning diesels on freight trains under wires energized to support the lion's share of the traffic in and out of New York City.

The FL9s, unique hybrid EMD diesels that ran on diesel power or used third-rail shoes to pick up power in third-rail territory, were purchased. Intended to spell the end of the catenary, the FL9s had lots of teething problems. They were used for passenger and occasional freight service, and several soldier on for Metro-North commuter railroad, some repainted in authentic New Haven McGinnis livery. But by 1963 the railroad trustees purchased 10 ex-Virginian EF-4 rectifier freight motors for use on Cedar Hill–Oak Point/Bay Ridge freights. They ran through the end of the New Haven and would see service in Penn Central black and Conrail blue.

The hopper cars barely visible to the right are indirectly powering No. 311 as it passes through Cos Cob. The hoppers carry coal for the generating station that powers the wires. The pagoda roof tower and the anchor bridge—the catenary bridge with all those transformers—are as New Haven as the EP-2. Photo by Fielding J. Bowman, June 6, 1952

Stamford was the original easternmost extent of the catenary. The boiler on EP-2 0325 is working overtime to heat this New York–Springfield, Massachusetts, train. Electric locomotives originally had a "0" prefix to prevent overlap with steam locomotive numbers. With the end of steam, the zeroes disappeared. Photo by Jim Bennett

From Stamford an eight-mile electrified branch headed to New Canaan. Heading this train is EP-1 016, one of the so-called "Ponies" built back in 1906 as the New Haven's first electric motors. Photo by Jim Bennett

The FL9s were introduced as part of McGinnis's de-electrification proposal. Happily, the wires outlasted McGinnis and his successors. Despite many initial problems, the FL9s proved themselves worthy and many still serve Metro-North today. Note the unique triangular catenary, a New Haven signature west of Stamford. Photo by Jim Shaughnessy

The main line crossed several navigable rivers on its run between New York and New Haven. Overhead wires did not run across this bridge. Electrics, like this one moving with a freight over the Cos Cob draw, had to coast across the bridge until the pantograph once again made contact with the wire. (Note the lack of wire to the left in this photo.) Photo by Jim Shaughnessy, February 24, 1958

Fashion *don't*? EP-2 No. 312 was one of four box-cabs (two EP-2s and two EP-3s) painted in the McGinnis colors white, black, and red. Certainly different, but nowhere near as attractive as the conservative green and yellow. Photo by Jim Shaughnessy, January 17, 1957

A long string of Osgood Bradley "American Flyer" coaches on New York–bound commuter train No. 365 pauses to take on passengers at Darien, Connecticut. The cars earned their nickname when The A. C. Gilbert Co. patterned their toy trains after them. No surprise, since Gilbert was a New Haven–based company. NYNH&H photo, July, 1947

Train No. 175, the Boston–Washington, D. C., *Patriot*, passes Greens Farms tower behind EP-5 No. 378. It will take this train to Penn Station, where it will be turned over to a Pennsy locomotive, very likely a GG1. Photo by John P. Ahrens, February 28, 1964

The light dusting of snow was no match for this trio of motors as they move a long freight westbound through Stratford, Connecticut. Photo by Kent W. Cochrane, January 1948

A perfectly matched set of green and yellow Alco cab units leads a westbound in electrified territory at West River, just west of New Haven. The train will leave the wires behind a few miles west of here at Devon, as it swings north through Derby Junction and into New York state on the Maybrook line. Photo by W. A. R. Edgecomb, June 30, 1953

Bridgeport provided the New Haven with lots of freight and passenger traffic throughout the 1950s. An eastbound to Boston stops with its solid consist of Pullman-Standard streamlined cars. Photo by John P. Ahrens, April 1952

These cars are sitting at Bridgeport on a 1965 fantrip, but this photo could have easily been taken 30 years earlier. Photo by Bill Meyers, July 4, 1965

EP-3: FORERUNNER TO A LEGEND

By the mid-1920s the New Haven's electric locomotive roster was dominated by Baldwin-Westinghouse units. Out of 126 electric locomotives on the roster, only eight were General Electric Products. After little success with seven EF-2/EY-3 class GE motor generators, which eliminated the quill drive required by larger AC traction motors, the New Haven returned to Baldwin-Westinghouse for quill drive power.

Engineers at General Electric returned to the drawing board and in 1931 combined quill drive, a proven winner on the New Haven, with twin AC motors mounted on a 2-C+C-2 wheel arrangement. The result, the New Haven's EP-3 class electric passenger motor, was possibly the most successful electric on the roster and quickly catapulted General Electric ahead of Baldwin-Westinghouse in the construction of heavy electric passenger equipment.

The EP-3s were completely new, since GE had built several look-alike motors for the Cleveland Union Terminal in 1929. But the locomotives built for CUT had single DC motors for each axle with no quill drive. The New Haven, which was never satisfied with the performance of DC power, preferred the AC arrangement that GE delivered.

Quickly nicknamed "Flatbottoms" by train crews, the big powerful electrics with their heavy sideframes and long porches overhanging the lead and trailing trucks hardly looked streamlined. Their slightly rounded ends, a departure from the typical GE perfectly blunt, flat end, gave the EP-3s a look more like that of their Baldwin-Westinghouse cousins. They were equipped with vertical steam boilers for heating passenger trains and third-rail shoes for operation in Grand Central Terminal.

At first, the EP-3s couldn't operate into New York's Penn Station. Instead, they turned their trains over to a Pennsy DD-1 in Sunnyside Yard. By 1933 the Pennsy's 11,000-volt AC electrification reached Penn Station, and the EP-3s were equipped with Pennsy cab signals for operation into the station proper. The ten EP-3s, the last boxcab-style electrics purchased by the New Haven, were numbered 0351–0360 (later renumbered 350–359). Capable of hauling fifteen 80-ton Pullman cars at speeds in excess of 70 miles per hour when built, they could reach 80 in the early 1940s after a regearing. The 56-inch drivers contributed to a starting tractive effort of 68,400 pounds, with a sustained tractive effort of 18,000 pounds.

The real fame of the EP-3s among railfans came, not in their original form on the New Haven, but in a slightly modified version built for the Pennsy, which would become the most famous electric locomotive ever built. Not satisfied with the performance of their P-5 class electrics, PRR borrowed at least three New Haven EP-3s (Nos. 0351, 0354, and 0359) and regeared them for 120 mph. Extensive testing over a two-year period and construction of an experimental electric based on the EP-3 convinced Pennsy officials that the EP-3's articulated truck frames and greater distribution of weight over axles (compared to the earlier P-5) tracked much better at higher speeds. The Pennsy essentially duplicated the EP-3's running gear and motors and, instead of a boxcab carbody, used a streamlined design. The famed GG1 was born.

Back on New Haven iron, the EP-3s soldiered on. Despite the fact that they had many good years left in them in the 1950s, they were victims of early retirement. A railroad management determined to eliminate overhead electrification in favor of diesel-electric hybrid FL9s, and the loss of passenger traffic to the Connecticut Turnpike, sealed their fate.

Two EP-3s (Nos. 355 and 358) lasted long enough to wear a variation of the McGinnis color scheme, two of only four boxcabs to be so decorated. These mighty electrics, built as shining stars of the high-speed passenger fleet, spent their last days on the Danbury branch working commuter runs. The 351 was the first of the class to be stricken from the roster in 1959, and by 1961 all ten were gone. Sadly, not a single example of this ground-breaking locomotive was preserved, although you can still see the heart of a New Haven EP-3 in any of the many preserved GG1s.

EP-3 0351 poses for its official portrait. If the running gear looks familiar, that's because the Pennsylvania Railroad borrowed EP-3s from the New Haven for testing. They were so impressed, they copied the running gear for their famed GG1s. General Electric photo, June 10, 1931

This aerial view shows the extent of the facilities operated in Bridgeport. Note the South Yard, roundhouse, and turntable. All are long gone today. Photo by Charles Obert, January 6, 1949

The EF-3bs were built as freight motors but could pinch-hit at Penn Station on New Haven passenger trains (lack of third-rail shoes kept them out of Grand Central). Dual-service capability was important on a railroad with short runs like the New Haven. Photo by John P. Ahrens, April, 1952

Electrified freight service returned to the New Haven with the 1963 purchase of ten Virginian Railway EF-4s. Here a pair of "Bricks" heads a freight through Greens Farms. The jumper is providing power to the unit with its "pan" down. Note the left-handed short blade semaphore, another NH trademark. Photo by John P. Ahrens, February 27, 1964

A set of FL9s on a New York–bound commuter train passes through Stamford on track one. Meanwhile, a set of M.U. cars, nicknamed "Washboards" because of their fluted sides, is stopped on track three. Photo by Jim Shaughnessy, May 1959

The terminus of the electrified portion of the Danbury branch was a loop track in front of the Danbury station. The station gained fame when it was used for a scene in the Alfred Hitchcock thriller *Strangers on a Train.* The EP-5, M.U. car, and wires are all gone. The station still stands and has been restored to house the Danbury Railroad Museum. Photo by J. W. Swanberg, May 9, 1959

Fairfield, Connecticut, is a bedroom community located on the New Haven main line. It was my home town, and I've looked at this scene many times. Here New York–bound train No. 71, behind a pair of FL9s, accelerates away from the station. Thanks to Metro-North, you can still see New Haven FL9s in Fairfield today. Photo by J. W. Swanberg, December 24, 1962

FL9: TRUE DIESEL ELECTRIC

The need to change from diesel to electric road power at New Haven was long a thorn in the New Haven's side. The dual-power locomotive, capable of running off the electrified third rail in New York City and on conventional diesel power, would mean eliminating the locomotive change at New Haven and would make it possible for the same locomotive to haul a train all the way from Penn Station or Grand Central to its final destination.

Dual-power locomotives were not unheard of. Several railroads, including the New York Central, had experimented with them as early as the 1920s. NYC had over 30 on its roster. But these were really electric locomotives designed to run for brief periods at reduced power when away from electrified territory. What the New Haven had in mind was a true hybrid—half diesel, half electric, capable of top-end performance in either situation.

While both Fairbanks-Morse and General Electric had toyed with designs in the early 1950s, no satisfactory solution could be found that met the weight restrictions on the Park Avenue viaduct in New York City.

After Patrick McGinnis acquired control of the New Haven, EMD proposed a modification of their FP9 passenger diesel that would meet the weight restrictions. McGinnis was very interested. He saw a chance to reap profits from the copper scrap value of the overhead wire, which the hybrid locomotive would make redundant. McGinnis was ousted before he could contract with EMD for the locomotives, but Alpert continued the McGinnis plans and ordered 60 of the locomotives from EMD before a single test model had been built.

EMD plans included installing its standard 1,750-hp diesel engine, with the addition of third-rail shoes to collect current when operating in New York. Designers felt there would be no problems in getting the third-rail pickup shoes to function, since the EMD power plant utilized 600 volts DC—the same voltage used on the third rail. The standard FP9 carbody was lengthened by 4 feet to accommodate additional control apparatus. To keep the axle loadings within the

Park Avenue viaduct limits a three-axle Flexicoil truck was used on the rear of the locomotive. The front truck was a standard two-axle Blomberg-style truck. A special shoe beam, which supported the third-rail pickup shoes, was installed on each side of the rear truck. No shoes were installed at first on the lead truck.

The first FL9s, Nos. 2000–2001, arrived in early 1957 and were complete flops. While the current rating of the FL9s was well within acceptable limits, the amperages that could be delivered if the third-rail shoe shorted out were tremendous. Often the 2,000-amp truck-side ribbon box fuses didn't act quickly enough and caused severe damage to the locomotives. In one instance, both demonstrators caught fire in third-rail territory and were returned to EMD.

The locomotives returned six months later with many improvements. The Blomberg front truck was replaced with a Flexicoil two-axle truck with front

pickup shoes installed. The roof included a small pantograph that the engineer could lower or raise to draw power from the overhead rail inside Grand Central Terminal. The New Haven finally accepted delivery of 2000–2001 in August 1957, and by the end of the year 2002 through 2029 were delivered. Plans for 60 units were shelved for a couple of years. FL9s Nos. 2030–2059 were delivered in 1960. By that time the F unit was considered passé, and New Haven No. 2059 was the last F of the 7,612 F units constructed by EMD.

The FL9s pushed many of the passenger electric locomotives—Fairbanks-Morse C-Liners and venerable DL109s—into retirement. Although the wire was removed from the Danbury branch, it soon became obvious to Alpert and his administration that the overhead wire represented a tremendous investment necessary for the commuter service. Running diesel-powered trains under already electrified wire was foolish. By the time this became apparent it was too late. An eleventh-hour effort to return the EF-3 electric freight motors to service even as the second order of FL9s was rolling onto the property proved hopeless. To no one's surprise, the New Haven slipped into bankruptcy in July 1961. Alpert's replacements quickly moved to acquire electric freight motors (EF-4s) from the Virginian.

Although acquiring the FL9s may not have been the best decision at the time, they have proved to be remarkably rugged locomotives. New Haven successors Penn Central and Conrail operated FL9s in former New Haven and New York Central territory. Amtrak acquired six units to cover trains in and out of Grand Central Terminal. Today, Metro-North commuter railroad utilizes a fleet of recently rebuilt FL9s on runs in both Connecticut and New York commuter territories.

Delivered in the McGinnis livery, the FL9s have worn a variety of paint schemes over the years, including Penn Central black, a unique blue and yellow paint scheme used by the New York Metropolitan Transit Authority in the early 1970s, and Metro-North's maroon, blue, and silver. But perhaps the most unusual thing to happen to the FL9s occurred in 1985, when four units owned by the Connecticut Department of Transportation, Nos. 2002, 2006, 2019, and 2023, were rebuilt and repainted in their original New Haven colors, complete with all New Haven markings. Six more were also repainted in NH colors in the 1990s. Those units and their 24 remaining sisters, despite the teething problems and ill timing of their early years, serve as a constant reminder of the New Haven railroad to thousands of commuters every day. Despite the arrival of Metro-North's new "Genesis" locomotives, which have third-rail capability, it's likely the FL9s will be around for years to come.

An EP-5, No. 378, has additional head-end cars for its New York–bound train. Its train, sitting out of view at the New Haven station, came from Boston behind diesels. The electric will take it the rest of the way to Penn Station.
Photo by Jim Shaughnessy

THE NEW HAVEN IN ITS HOMETOWN

The city of New Haven, located halfway between the New York and Rhode Island state lines on the Connecticut coast, was the heart of the New Haven Railroad. With its extensive yard facilities, shops, and locomotive-servicing facilities that serviced steam, electric, and diesel motive power, New Haven is worth a detailed look.

Lines to many points on the railroad converged in New Haven. The main line to New York, the Shore Line to Boston, and the line to Maybrook all originated from New Haven. In addition, a line headed north to both Hartford and Springfield, Massachusetts.

Passenger facilities

The first stations in the city were built prior to the Civil War to serve the various predecessor companies, including the New York & New Haven. By the 1860s a Union Station had been constructed on Chapel Street. That station was replaced by a much larger brick station at the foot of Meadow Street, which succumbed to fire in May 1918. It was replaced with the structure that opened on April 5, 1920, and served the New Haven until the Penn Central takeover.

All passenger trains stopped at New Haven, and it was here that any trains heading into New York City took part in the time-honored ritual of exchanging their steam or diesel locomotives for electrics. Likewise, trains outbound from New York exchanged their electric locomotives for steam or diesel power. To save time, the motive power changes took place while the trains sat at the station loading and unloading passengers. Also, coaches, diners, parlor cars, and head-end (baggage and express) cars were added to or removed from trains. Some trains required more work than others, depending on the type of service, time of day, and route they followed.

There were ten through tracks in New Haven station—not small, but certainly not anywhere near the size of Boston's South Station or the terminals in New York City. Eight of the through tracks had platforms, and the remaining two were for through traffic. Four mainline tracks that headed east were double-signaled, permitting four movements in either direction at the same time.

Locomotive-servicing facilities

There were two main locomotive-servicing areas in New Haven. Just west of the station were motor storage and servicing facilities for locomotives used for mainline and Springfield line passenger trains. A much larger facility was located alongside the New York/Maybrook freight departure yard in Cedar Hill, just north of New Haven.

Upon arrival a diesel locomotive was inspected at the pit and given any necessary running repairs, after which it headed to the ready track to await its next outbound assignment. Locomotives needing more extensive repair work were sent to the shop. In the 1950s, approximately 125 electric and diesel locomotives were readied by the Cedar Hill engine facility every day.

Cedar Hill freight yards

The Cedar Hill freight yards sprawled over 880 acres alongside the Quinnipiac River just north of New Haven. The yards consisted of 25 individual yards and switching districts and contained 154 miles of track. Cedar Hill measured 7.4 miles from north to south and approximately 1.5 miles from east to west.

The names of the most significant component yards are fairly self-explanatory: New York/Maybrook Receiving, New York/Maybrook Departure, Shore Line Receiving, Shore Line Departure, North and Eastbound Departure, and Southbound Receiving. Cars were placed in trains ready to depart from these yards. Classification, or switching, took place at one of the two major classification yards. These were gravity hump yards, meaning that a cut of cars was slowly shoved up a hill (humped) and uncoupled at the crest. From there the cars rolled down to the appropriate classification track. Car speed was controlled by air retarders, air jets that produced short blasts of compressed air to control a car's speed. The classification yards each had 51 double-ended tracks with a capacity of 1,700 cars. A hump yard was much faster than a conventional "flat" yard. The Cedar Hill hump was capable of classifying 100 loaded cars in 25 minutes. Once the cars had been sorted by destination onto a single classification track they were transferred to the departure yards.

Switcher 0906 is working a cut of passenger cars in November 1940. Built by General Electric in 1940, this Ingersol-Rand–powered locomotive predated the arrival of the DL109s by a full year. The building to the right was the railroad's general office building. Photo by Charles H. Grabert, November 1940

Much of the sprawling Cedar Hill is visible here. Note the dual roundhouses and coaling tower in left center. Westbound departure tracks for Maybrook and New York City are left of the engine facilities. The eastbound arrival yard passes to the right of the engine facilities, leading to the two classification yards, along with the less-than-carload sheds, in the distance. Photo by E. R. Meaker, October 1, 1948

Passengers enjoy an evening meal in the diner *Myles Standish* as the *Merchants Limited* sits in New Haven before resuming its trip to Boston. The picture was taken from a coach seat in the New York–Montreal *Ambassador*. Photo by Wallace W. Abbey, August 26, 1953

A clean EP-5 No. 378 has the highball and departs New Haven station with yet another train for New York City. 1955-built GE electrics introduced the McGinnis scheme to the railroad. Photo by Jim Shaughnessy

The fireman climbs down from Alco FA-1 0408 at the Cedar Hill terminal. Fairbanks-Morse C-Liner No. 795 shows off its McGinnis scheme while DL109 0706, like the FAs, wears classic green and yellow colors. Photo by Jim Shaughnessy, July 13, 1956

A set of DL109s in pinstripe livery, led by the 0704, get fuel, water, and sand at the New Haven engine terminal. The next assignment could be a Shore Line freight or perhaps a Springfield passenger train for these dual-service units.
NYNH&H photo

Looks like 1941-built 0705 is giving the evil eye to a newly arrived Alco cousin RS-11, No. 1412. Once the engines are prepared for their next runs, "turned" in railroad parlance, they will take trains to Boston. Photo by Jim Shaughnessy, July 13, 1956

The fireman wipes down I-5 No. 1405 alongside the massive Cedar Hill coaling tower on a rainy day. This "Shoreliner" will take the *Yankee Clipper* to Boston. Photo by H. W. Pontin

Railroading is a 24-hour-a-day business. Alco RS-11s (New Haven class DERS-5) were an unplanned purchase when EMD couldn't deliver 120 GP9s in 1956. The railroad settled for 30 GP9s, 15 RS-11s, and 15 Fairbanks-Morse H-16-44s instead. Photo by Jim Shaughnessy, June 20, 1960

A perfectly matched A-B-A set of Alco FA-1s, resplendent in orange and green with gray pinstripes, prepares to leave the Westbound departure yard with a Maybrook-bound freight. NYNH&H photo, September 1947

A Y-4 class 0-8-0 switcher, the 3605, smokes up the wires in Cedar Hill. Note the brakeman on the refrigerator car roof. Photo by H. W. Pontin, 1935

Number 0616, an Alco S-2, pushes a short cut over the Eastbound hump. New Haven S-2s had low-clearance cab roofs, making them noticeably less rounded than S-2s built for other roads. Photo by E. R. Meaker, October 22, 1948

An L-1 2-10-2 is on the point with R-1a 4-8-2 No. 3338 as road engine as the two prepare to cut off their train on the arrival tracks. The train is just in from Fall River, Massachusetts, and the two locomotives will head for the Cedar Hill engine terminal. Photo by E. R. Meaker, October 13, 1948

Bumped from passenger service by diesels, an I-4 class Pacific, the 1387, pushes an eastbound freight into the tunnel at East Haven, Connecticut. Photo by Kent Cochrane, July 4, 1947

A trio of Alco road freight units is entering Cedar Hill with a manifest from the Boston & Maine connection at Worcester, Massachusetts. Photo by E. R. Meaker

One of the New Haven's 30 GP9s sits at Cedar Hill awaiting its next assignment. The 1200 was the first of a planned 120-unit GP9 fleet that would have replaced all the road diesels on the line. "Cadillacs," as the Geeps were nicknamed, were popular with crews, but money-short New Haven never carried out the all-EMD plan. NYNH&H photo, September 9, 1960

A perfectly matched A-B-A set of Alco road cab units leads a long Maybrook-bound freight. These 1947 sets and their five additional FB-2 sisters replaced the 50 2-10-2s that once dominated the Maybrook line.
Photo by Frank W. Schlegel

Maybrook Line: Freight artery

The Maybrook Line started at Derby Junction, Connecticut, just west of Milford. From there, it ran west through Danbury, Conn., and continued west across the New York state line and up Poughquag Hill, a 1.34 percent grade. From the summit of the hill trains descended a 14-mile-long, 1.15 percent grade into Hopewell Junction.

West of Hopewell Junction was the Poughkeepsie Bridge, a 6,768-foot span that crossed 212 feet over the Hudson River, one of the most spectacular railroad bridges in the eastern United States. Once safely over the bridge, trains traveled upgrade another 20 miles into Maybrook itself.

Maybrook played host to the New Haven and the Erie, Lehigh & Hudson River, Lehigh & New England, and the New York, Ontario & Western railroads. Three miles west of Maybrook, at Campbell Hall, the New Haven interchanged with the NYC's Wallkill Valley line.

At Maybrook the New Haven maintained a large freight yard, as well as locomotive-servicing facilities. There were both east- and westbound classification yards, each one with its own hump. Since the hump yards weren't equipped with automatic retarders, brakemen had to ride cars down the hump and control car speed using the handbrakes.

By 1914 the entire Maybrook line was double-tracked. Passenger service, except for the occasional fantrip, ended in 1927. Since the Maybrook Line was the closest the New Haven ever got to mountain railroading, pusher, or helper, operations were a frequent sight during the steam era.

For many years the Maybrook line was the stomping ground of the New Haven's 50 L-1 class 2-10-2s. In 1947 these locomotives were replaced by 15 A-B-A sets of Alco freight cab units. Pusher operations became rare, although for a while an RS-3 would be assigned to push out of Hopewell Junction if a train's tonnage required it—at least until the A-B-A sets were augmented with new B units in 1951, which permitted the operation of four-unit sets on the Maybrook line.

With the decline in freight traffic the line was single-tracked between Highland and Maybrook. By 1961 the entire route was single-tracked.

The Maybrook line outlasted the New Haven, but not by much. While under Penn Central ownership, the famed Poughkeepsie Bridge suffered a fire in 1974. The bridge was closed to traffic and the Maybrook line, a redundant route in the Conrail era, is no more.

Between Derby Junction and Devon, Connecticut, the Naugatuck and Maybrook lines shared the same eight-mile stretch. At Turkey Brook, an R-2 class 4-8-2 No. 3500 drags a Cedar Hill–Waterbury freight. The R-2 was the only member of its class, basically an R-1b with a heavier boiler. The diesel-powered freight is heading for New Haven from Maybrook. Photo by Kent W. Cochrane

L-1 class 2-10-2 No. 3228 has a long Maybrook-bound freight as it passes through Newtown, Connecticut. No. 3228 and its 49 sisters were ideal for handling tonnage on the Maybrook line. Photo by N. Netherbee

The 3232 is working hard and putting out lots of coal smoke as it heads AO-9, the Hartford-to-Maybrook freight, through Newington. Photo by Kent W. Cochrane, May 23, 1948

Alco cab units pass the soon-to-be-passé water tank at the east end of the Danbury Fairgrounds. Even without the date on the back of the photo, it's easy to judge from the shine that these units are brand new. Photo by John P. Ahrens, August 8, 1947

A yellow-trimmed FA-1, the 0400, leads an eastbound freight through Danbury in this pan shot.
Photo by J. W. Swanberg, 1954

In Danbury the Maybrook line connected with the electrified branch to Norwalk. Here the wire train is sitting on the balloon, or loop, track in front of Danbury station. The station is now the home of the Danbury Railroad Museum. Photo by Kent W. Cochrane, September 1947

L-1 class 2-10-2 No. 3235 trails OB-2 (Maybrook to Boston) up the ruling grade on the Maybrook line through Poughquag, New York. A second 2-10-2 is pushing on the rear. This was one of the last steam runs on the Maybrook line. Photo by John P. Ahrens, September 1, 1947

One hundred cars back from the 3235 we see No. 3217 shoving hard on the tail end of eastbound OB-2. Photo by John P. Ahrens, September 1, 1947

A wartime freight passes through Whaley Lake, New York, tacked on the drawbar of No. 3227. Photo by John P. Ahrens, August 1942

Road switchers from three builders, an Alco RS-11, an EMD GP9, and a Fairbanks-Morse H-16-44s, depart Maybrook with a Boston-bound freight. The New Haven mixed diesel units freely, with little regard for manufacturer or model. Photo by Gene Collora, May 29, 1960

The bovine residents of Fishkill Plains, New York, don't even give the Alcos a second glance as the locomotives pass through a pastoral scene with a manifest freight. Photo by Jim Shaughnessy, September 10, 1956

It was unusual to find Alco DL109s on the Maybrook line. These units usually stayed on flatter territory. Two of them, Nos. 0739 and 0747, climb the hill at Greenhaven, New York. A 2-10-2 is pushing on the rear. Photo by John P. Ahrens, July 12, 1947

No passenger trains have stopped at Hopewell Junction since 1927, but the windows are still rattled by long freights, like NO-7 (New Haven to Maybrook). The train is westbound for the Poughkeepsie Bridge and Maybrook, where most of its cars will go to the Erie. Photo by Jim Shaughnessy, May 15, 1957

The tall bridge over the Hudson River at Poughkeepsie, New York, was the scenic highlight of the Maybrook line. A long westbound freight crosses the bridge, obeying the 12 mph speed limit. Photo by Kent W. Cochrane

This time we're looking down from the caboose on freight OB-4 as it passes over the New York Central's yard at Poughkeepsie. This viewpoint shows how much of the span is over land, not water. Photo by Wallace W. Abbey

A Lima-Hamilton switcher works a cut of reefers in Maybrook yard. The photographer was standing in the caboose of Maybrook-to-Boston OB-4 as it awaited clearance to depart. Photo by Wallace W. Abbey, March 1952

Power for the eastbound hump was this pair of Lima-Hamilton DEY-6 class switchers. These two were part of a series of ten locomotives built in 1950. They were painted warm orange with black "New Haven" hood lettering, and their cabs were green with orange script lettering. Photo by Wallace W. Abbey, March 1952

Here's what the engine-servicing facilities looked like in Maybrook before the arrival of diesels. It won't be long before 3240 will leave town on the point of a freight bound for Cedar Hill or Boston. Photo by Pierre M. Ditto, October 1940

The Shore Line was the stomping ground of the I-5s. The *Bostonian* is eastbound through Shore Line Junction, just outside Cedar Hill, behind the 1407. Note the block "New Haven" lettering on the tender. Photo by John P. Ahrens, April 1938

The Shore Line

According to the New Haven's public timetables, the Shore Line was the route between New York City and Boston, Massachusetts. But to New Haven employees and fans the term "Shore Line" referred to the route between New Haven and Boston, along the tracks that partly belonged to the Shore Line Railroad, one of the New Haven's nineteenth-century predecessors.

The Shore Line began at Shore Line Junction, just east of Cedar Hill Yard in New Haven. Despite the name, the Shore Line didn't really run within sight of the coast for its entire length. Instead, it skirted the coast of Long Island Sound through southern Connecticut until it reached Rhode Island. Once in Rhode Island, the main line swung north to pass through the cities of Kingston and Providence. Several lines emanated from Providence to serve Bristol, Pascoag, and, via Valley Falls, the industrial city of Worcester, Mass. A branch from Attleboro also headed south to serve Newport, a fine natural harbor and a playground for the well-to-do since the late 1800s.

The Shore Line was double-tracked for its entire length. Over the years it saw only the finest and fastest power on the railroad, from the streamlined I-5 class 4-6-4s, christened "Shoreliners" on the NH, to the DL109s and famed Alco PA1s.

Since the Shore Line was a relatively short run, dual-service capability was a priority for all motive power. This requirement was the main reason the New Haven purchased dual-service DL109s and PA-1s from Alco and passed up the E and F units other railroads were gobbling up in the postwar years as fast as EMD's factory at La Grange, Illinois, could turn them out. Diesel locomotives, unlike their more specialized steam-powered counterparts, regularly pulled passenger trains during the day and freight trains by night. While there were certainly freights along the Shore Line in daylight, and passenger trains after dark, as a rule the passenger trains dominated during daylight hours. New Haven management was thrilled when DL-109s or PA-1s could arrive in South Station with a passenger train and, within an hour, be heading back to New Haven on the point of a long freight.

Even more so than the electrified west end, the Shore Line was the New Haven's racetrack. It was a place to let passenger trains do what they did best—run at speed.

R-1-b class 4-8-2 3343 is eastbound at East Haven, Connecticut. The New Haven found that 4-8-2s, like this 1924 Alco product, were ideal steam power for Shore Line fast freight service. Photo by Kent W. Cochrane

A westbound Shore Line freight stretches into the distance behind R-1-a class 4-8-2 No. 3311 just east of Cedar Hill yard. Model railroaders should note the variety of car types and styles in this train. NYNH&H photo taken from tower SS81

There's no lack of smoke and steam as Shoreliner No. 1402 heads train No. 12, the *Bay State,* east to Boston through Pine Orchard, Connecticut. Basic black with chrome silver accents provided just a touch of class without being gaudy. Photo by John P. Ahrens, February 23, 1948

Train No. 174, the *Colonial,* has an all–New Haven consist this day. Teaming up Alco PA-1s and Fairbanks-Morse C-Liners wasn't uncommon on New Haven passenger runs. Photo by David Plowden, November 1954

Someone took extra care when they lined up the ballast edge. We're at Stony Creek, watching an eastbound freight roar past behind 4-8-2 No. 3318. Sadly, the 3318 met the scrapper's torch three months after this photo was taken. No New Haven steam locomotives have been preserved. Photo by Kent W. Cochrane

A pair of F-M H-16-44s, Baby TrainMasters, are less than two weeks old as they lead a Boston-bound passenger train through Branford, Connecticut. Photo by Jim Shaughnessy, September 10, 1956

A pair of Alco DL-109s puts some characteristic smoke in the air as it passes Shore Line Junction with Maybrook-to-Boston freight OB-8 in tow. The pair will take the train on the last leg of its trip to Boston. Photo by E. R. Meaker, October 31, 1948

One of the line's 50 I-4 class Pacifics, No. 1370, blasts through Guilford, Connecticut, with the *Park Avenue Special* in tow. No. 1370 was the only I-4 equipped with an experimental cast-steel smokebox. Photo by John P. Ahrens, March 9, 1941

Another R-class 4-8-2, the 3500, has a long string of empties in tow as it departs Cedar Hill for the Central Vermont connection in New London. Those empties will be on their way north before long as part of a CV train to Montreal, Canada. Photo by E. R. Meaker

The Connecticut River was spanned by this long drawbridge between Saybrook and Lyme. The draw span is raised to let waterborne traffic through. Photo by W. A. R. Edgecomb

The Shore Line crossed another large drawbridge over the Thames River between New London and Groton. The train is following the Shore Line route to Boston. The tracks curving to the right form the Worcester line to Worcester, Massachusetts. Photo by Wayne Brumbaugh, September 3, 1948

A pair of DL109s crosses the Thames River into Groton, Connecticut. The tall bridge in the background is the Gold Star Bridge, which carried U.S. Route 1 (now the Interstate 95 bridge). It will contribute a great deal to the loss of New Haven freight and passenger traffic in the near future. NYNH&H photo, July 1, 1952

Freight extra 3323, running from Cedar Hill to Boston, steps off the Thames River bridge into Groton. Photo by Wayne Brumbaugh, June 22, 1949

It's Labor Day weekend and traffic is heavy. An I-5 class 4-6-4 has the *Colonial,* train No. 175, heading towards New York and Washington, D. C. Here it's passing the Groton tower. Sure looks more enjoyable than sitting in traffic! Photo by Wayne Brumbaugh, September 3, 1948

Busy day at Kingston, Rhode Island. The westbound *Gilt Edge* behind a set of DL-109s accelerates out of the station as a set of PA-1s on the Boston-bound *Colonial* arrives on the right. The RS-1 and caboose belong to the Providence–New London local freight, which is working several sidings until things quiet down on the main. Photo by Bob Milner, September 1950

The dome of the Rhode Island state capitol building is visible to the left as a Boston–New York passenger run passes through Providence behind a pair of DL-109s. NYNH&H photo, September 1954

An RS-3–powered freight crosses the Sakonnet River onto Aquidneck Island on its way to Newport, Rhode Island. The flatcars are carrying a pair of EMD MP-36 power units for use by Newport Electric Co. Photo by Bruce Meyer, October 26, 1960

The Willimantic-to-Boston *Morning Express* is about to end its run behind a green and yellow PA-1. The consist on the left is backing across the Fort Point Channel drawbridges. It will leave bound for Grand Central as the *Clocker*.
Photo by W. G. Fancher, October 26, 1950

The New Haven in Boston

Boston, the unofficial capital of New England and one of the most important cities in the region, was an appropriate eastern terminus for the New Haven. Boston was founded as a port city and for many years was one of the most important harbors along the eastern seaboard. It was also a longtime banking and manufacturing capital. All these factors contributed to making "Beantown" an important rail center.

Most of the New Haven's lines in eastern Massachusetts were acquired as part of the Old Colony line. The Old Colony dated back to 1845, when a line was opened between Boston and Plymouth, Mass. In 1854 the Old Colony was merged with the Fall River Railroad, which dated back to an 1845 consolidation of three smaller lines that linked Fall River with a connection with the Old Colony at Braintree. By 1883 the Old Colony merged the Boston, Clinton, Fitchburg & New Bedford, which extended from the famed whaling port of New Bedford to Fitchburg. In 1888 the Old Colony incorporated the Boston & Providence. This gave the Old Colony a connection with the New Haven in Providence.

In 1893 the New Haven leased the Old Colony, effectively doubling the size of the parent line and gaining access to Boston and the rich industrial cities in eastern Massachusetts and Rhode Island.

South Station

Boston's South Station, located at the corner of Summer Street and Atlantic Avenue, was the busiest railroad station in North America from the time it opened in 1899 until it was superseded by Grand Central Terminal almost three decades later.

Prior to the opening of South Station four separate terminals served the railroads coming in from the south and west of Boston. A special Rapid Transit Commission was appointed in 1892 to find a solution to the growing overcrowding in all the city's railroad terminals. The commission recommended the construction of union stations, one in the northern part of the city, the second in the southern part.

Construction commenced on the new South Station in 1896. More than 200 buildings were removed to make room for the station and its approaches and tracks. Unlike the stations in New York City, most of the platform tracks in Boston were above ground, although several loop, or balloon, tracks were included for turning electric trains (which never materialized). The station was completed on December 31, 1898, at a cost of $3.6 million.

Originally the station included a 570 x 602-foot train shed with a steel and glass roof. The train shed was removed in 1930 when repairs to the structure would have proved too costly. At the same time, the station received a $2.5 million facelift. The train shed was replaced by umbrella-style platform roofs.

South Station saw a period of considerable decline, and at one point was in danger of being torn down entirely. A section of the Dorchester Avenue end was removed in 1973. By this time people realized the historical significance of the main station building and its potential value as a renovated transportation center. Today, the completely renovated South Station serves as a shopping destination, as well as travel hub, for Bostonians and those arriving from elsewhere. Like a growing number of massive railroad stations, South Station's usefulness has far outlasted the grim demise predicted for it in the early 1970s.

Traffic and operations

In addition to serving as a major east-end passenger terminal of the New Haven, Boston also played host to a large freight terminal. The South Boston Freight Yard and the Dover Street passenger yards classified thousands of cars daily.

As always, passenger traffic, in volumes that seem unimaginable today, was an important part of the New Haven in Boston. In 1954, 318 trains entered and departed South Station every day. The New Haven had a total of 235 and the Boston & Albany 83. The New Haven's trains ranged from lowly locals and commuter runs over the lines of the Old Colony and the main line to Providence, or the branches emanating from Boston to Needham, Franklin, and Stoughton, Mass., to name trains that called on South Station. The B&A dispatched the *New England States Limited* and the Boston section of its NYC parent's famed *20th Century*.

The New Haven saw almost hourly departures and arrivals of manifest passenger trains such as the *Merchants Limited* and the *Yankee Clipper* for New York City, and the *Senator* and *Colonial* for Washington, D. C., by way of Penn Station and the Pennsylvania Railroad.

To prepare and classify the hundreds of cars needed for this level of service the New Haven maintained Dover Street Yards, actually a large complex of yards across the Fort Point Channel from South Station.

Like their passenger counterparts, all types of freight trains, from lowly way freights to scheduled manifests, departed and arrived in Boston. Some terminated here, but many loads were eventually passed on to the Boston & Maine for delivery to points farther north. Trains BH-7 and HB-8 operated between Boston and the Harlem River Yard in New York City with a large percentage of piggyback traffic. Most of the scheduled freight movements into Boston were eastbound. Westbound traffic was nowhere near as heavy, reflecting the New Haven's perpetual handicap as a terminating line. That meant the road made money on inbound traffic, but westbound freight movements were typically unscheduled, or extra moves, and yardmasters filled tonnage of westbound trains with empty cars returning to their point of origin.

South Boston freight yard, with its myriad of classification tracks and freight houses for transferring less-than-carload (LCL) cargo from rail cars to trucks, was adjacent to Dover Street Yards; at one point one of the yards in Dover Street complex was used as a produce terminal for fresh fruit, meat, and vegetables.

South Station in Boston from street level. Despite threatened condemnation, the famed facade still stands and serves Amtrak and Boston commuters today. NYNH&H photo

The joint Pennsy–New Haven *Colonial* between Boston and Washington, D. C., departs from South Station with its all-Pennsy consist. The Parlor-Lounge-Observation car *Alexander Hamilton* carries the markers. Photo by Scott Andrews, December 1966

Locomotive utilization was critical, so dual-purpose locomotives were favored by the NH. These Alco DL109s typically pulled the varnish by day and lugged freight by night. This dual-service versatility was critical to keeping the traffic moving during the record years of World War II. NYNH&H photo

A DL109 bears down on a Boston & Albany 4-6-4, just about to pass under the landmark signal bridge. Yet another train is moving to our left. NYNH&H photo

Having just arrived from one of its last revenue trips, I-4 class Pacific No. 1380 backs to the enginehouse. South Station's intricate trackwork presents a true challenge to model railroaders! Photo by W. G. Fancher, October 26, 1950

No. 1335 steams eastbound with a passenger train, very likely a commuter run, while a set of DL109s departs westbound with *The Senator* in tow. Photo by Albert G. Hale, March 20, 1946

The new building looming in the background is the Post Office. South Station is the darker brick structure in the distance. The brand-new Fairbanks-Morse C-Liner No. 792 is tied onto the front end of the Pennsy's equally new Budd-built *Senator*. Photo by Parker Hayden, April 2, 1952

Back Bay is the first station out of South Station. The John Hancock tower, prior to the construction of the reflective glass tower, looms in the background. PA-1 0783 prepares to depart with the *Yankee Clipper.* C. Parker, March 2, 1952

The New Haven was an early experimenter with piggyback operations. A string of flatcars is being unloaded "circus" style at South Boston. Completion of the interstate highway between New York and Boston eventually cost the New Haven much of its early piggyback business. Photo by Jim Phelan, August 11, 1952

Alco 600-horsepower switcher 0924, built in 1940, works a cut of cars at Commonwealth Pier. Alco switchers were longtime residents of Boston. Photo by Jim Shaughnessy, January 5, 1963

A pair of Alco warbaby DL109s leads a passenger extra (note the white flag) through Bridgewater, Massachusetts, on Labor Day weekend. Photo by Wayne Brumbaugh, year unknown

I-4 No. 1399 smokes it up through Worcester, Massachusetts, on the point of a mixed train. Note the Brookside milk car behind the tender. Photo by H. F. Harvey, March 1944

The *Merchants Limited,* the country's first all-parlor train, races through Sharon, Massachusetts, behind a glistening I-5 Shoreliner sometime before 1948. Photo by Wayne Brumbaugh

The local passenger run pulls into the neat brick station at Sharon behind a trim I-4. This train is bound for Providence, Rhode Island. Photo by C. Parker, October 18, 1947

The New Haven's fleet of I-class 4-6-2s made its last stand on commuter runs in and around Boston. Here a pair of I-2s, built in 1913, meets just north of Braintree during the morning rush hour. Both these engines would meet the scrapper by year's end, but sisters 1312 and 1318 would be two of the New Haven's last active steam locomotives. Photo by Kent Cochrane, March 1948

A local pulls through Braintree, Massachusetts, after a blizzard has dumped plenty of white stuff. Note the old Look Out for the Engine crossing sign, once a common sight throughout New England. NYNH&H photo, January 1947

Fresh out of the Readville Shops, I-5 No. 1402 speeds across the ancient stone viaduct at Canton, Massachusetts. No. 1402, and its nine sisters, all built by Baldwin in 1937, were the only streamlined steamers built for a New England railroad. Photo by Kent Cochrane, February 1948

The South Shore Club observation car was bumped from the *Merchants Limited* when the Pullman stainless-steel cars were delivered. The car was charted by a group of Old Colony line commuters. Here it passes through Weymouth, Massachusetts, carrying the markers for train No. 675. NYNH&H photo, June 7, 1950

A pair of DL109s, with the New York–Cape Cod *Cape Codder* in tow, threads through the largest vertical lift bridge in the world, which spans the Cape Cod Canal at Buzzards Bay, Massachusetts. The bridge was built by the U. S. Army Corps of Engineers and is maintained by them today. Photo by Wayne P. Ellis

The line split once it crossed the Cape Cod Canal bridge. One line went to Woods Hole, shown here with a quartet of RDCs waiting to board passengers. This was once an important transfer point between the trains and ferries to Nantucket and Martha's Vineyard. Photo by B. J. Cudahy, July 1957

From Buzzards Bay a second line once headed around the long arm of Cape Cod all the way to Provincetown. A pair of FL9s has the *Day Cape Codder* in tow. By the time this picture was taken, passengers took the train to Hyannis, with a bus connection to Provincetown. Photo by R. Ingram, July 1964

"New Haven" No. 2002, owned by the Connecticut Department of Transportation, passes through Stamford, Conn., on Train No. 1839. The locomotive is pushing the train and is moving away from the photographer. The car wash building is to the left. Photo by J. W. Swanberg, July 24, 1995

The New Haven today

The New York, New Haven & Hartford ceased to exist as a corporate entity on midnight, December 31, 1968, when the lines that constituted the New Haven were merged into Penn Central, a company that had been formed from the ailing New York Central and Pennsylvania Railroads only a year before.

Since it served such a densely populated region of the country, the New Haven avoided complete abandonment. But changes were still fast and overwhelmingly apparent to those who witnessed them first hand. Electric motors on freights were no more as Penn Central transferred the former New Haven EF-4s to lines formerly operated by the Pennsylvania Railroad. And more vestiges of the former PRR appeared on the New Haven. Pennsy GG1s bumped the EP-5s onto commuter runs. Likewise, E8s still wearing Pennsy Tuscan red took over the Shore Line routes from the FL9s—sending the latter into suburban service on former New York Central and NH lines.

Penn Central tried to make a go of passenger service between New York and Boston, hiring car cleaners to try to make the trains more appealing. The oldest equipment was scrapped, and railfans mourned the loss of even the gaudy McGinnis colors as they disappeared under PC black.

The NYC-PRR-NH merger was anything but a match made in heaven. With duplicate routes, traffic-routing computers that couldn't talk to each other, large numbers of highly unprofitable passenger routes, and duplicate resources and personnel at all levels, Penn Central seemed certain to fail. The inevitable happened a little later as Penn Central declared it was insolvent—the largest corporate bankruptcy in U. S. history until that time.

While the preceding may lead one to believe that railroading in the Northeast has been one disaster after another, the story is a little brighter than that. After the PC failure, government agencies took over both local and long-distance passenger operations, eliminating the biggest drain on the New Haven. Today Metro-North operates commuter service in and out of New York City, using some former New Haven FL9s repainted in McGinnis colors. The Massachusetts Bay Transportation Authority (MBTA) handles Boston's commuter needs. Boston South Station has been refurbished with shops and restaurants geared toward serving commuters and shoppers, and Grand Central in New York is undergoing a similar renovation. Long-distance passenger trains no longer call on Grand Central, but Amtrak, which took over intercity passenger travel in 1971, continues to run along the Shore Line between New York's Penn Station and Boston. And New Haven still sees the classic change of motive power from electric to diesel as it has for nearly a century.

Freight service on the old New Haven lines has also undergone significant change. The Consolidated Rail Corporation (Conrail) took over the PC and several other unprofitable and bankrupt Northeastern roads on April 1, 1976. With a Federal bailout and a Congressional mandate to make a profit, Conrail had the power to abandon or sell many unprofitable or duplicate lines, power lacked by its predecessors. Many of the New Haven's old branches and secondary lines were sold to smaller regional or shortline railroads, abandoned altogether, or returned to the state, which then donated them to railroad groups interested in museums. These museums and steam railroads—most notably the Valley Railroad in Essex, Connecticut, the Danbury Railroad Museum in Danbury, and the Railroad Museum of New England in Waterbury—pass on the heritage of this once-great New England institution for future generations. Small freight railroads, like the Housatonic, have shown that it is possible to operate a successful railroad in today's environment in New England. While there may be less track and fewer paint schemes today, people still depend on the tracks built by the New York, New Haven & Hartford to get to and from work, travel on vacations, or ship finished goods and raw materials.

In many ways the old New Haven railroad is still alive and well today. It couldn't have a better legacy than that.

Acknowledgments

When I was approached about compiling a Golden Years book on an eastern railroad, the New Haven immediately jumped to mind. For years I've considered the New Haven my hometown railroad. Even though it had disappeared into Penn Central when I was four years old, the tracks, much of the equipment, and, most important, the people I saw trackside as a youngster considered themselves and everything around them to be "New Haven." Two former New Haven employees, Rick Abramson and J. W. "Jack" Swanberg, proofread my copy. I'm honored to be able to call these men my friends, and the finished work is much better because of their efforts. Any mistakes are mine, not Jack's or Rick's. Jack also came through at the last minute and provided several of his own photos to supplement those on file at Kalmbach. I would be remiss if I didn't thank all the photographers who submitted their work to Kalmbach Publishing Co. Without them and hundreds of others like them, there would be no Golden Years of Railroading series.

Finally, I'd like to dedicate this book to John McGuirk. Though not a railfan or model railroader himself, he has always found the time to support and appreciate my interests. This one's for you, Dad.

INDEX OF PHOTOGRAPHS

Locations
Aquidneck Island: 99
Back Bay: 110
Boston: 111, 112
Boston (South Station): 100, 103–109
Braintree: 117, 118
Branford: 89
Bridgeport: 39, 42, 43
Bridgewater: 113
Buzzards Bay: 121, 123
Canton: 119
Cos Cob: 30, 33
Danbury: 44, 69, 70, 71
Darien: 35
East Haven: 61, 84
Fairfield: 45
Fishkill Plains: 75
Greenhaven: 76
Greens Farms: 36, 43
Groton: 94–96
Hopewell Junction: 77
Kingston: 97
Maybrook: 74, 80, 81
New Haven: cover, 51–61, 63, 92
New Rochelle: 19
Newington: 68
Newtown: 67
New York City: 19, 22
New York City (Grand Central Terminal): 12, 16, 21
New York City (Hell Gate Bridge): 23–26
New York City (Pennsylvania Station): 27
Pine Orchard: 86
Port Chester: 18
Poughkeepsie: 78, 79
Poughquag: 72
Providence: 98
Saybrook: 93
Sharon: 115, 116
Shore Line Junction: 82, 85, 90
Stamford: 31, 44, 124
Stoney Creek: 88
Stratford: 37
Turkey Brook: 66
West Haven: 28
Weymouth: 120
Whaley Lake: 73
Woodlawn Junction: 16
Woods Hole: 122
Worcester: 114

Diesel locomotives
C-Liner No. 792: 109
C-Liner No. 795: 53
DL-109 No. 0701: 105
DL-109 No. 0704: 54
DL-109 No. 0705: 55
DL-109 No. 0706: 53
DL-109 No. 0708: 121
DL-109 No. 0729: 97
DL-109 No. 0739: 76
DL-109 No. 0742: 94
DL-109 No. 0743: 94
DL-109 No. 0744: 108
DL-109 No. 0747: 76
FA-1 No. 0400: 70
FA-1 No. 0403: 58
FA-1 No. 0406: 64
FA-1 No. 0408: 53, 69
FA-1 No. 0412: 77
FA-1 No. 0413: 38
FA-1 No. 0422: 62
FB-1 No. 0451: 58
FB-1 No. 0455: 38
FL9 No. 2000: 46
FL9 No. 2001: 46
FL9 No. 2002: 124
FL9 No. 2014: 48
FL9 No. 2017: 12
FL9 No. 2018: 44, 45
FL9 No. 2029: 32
FL9 No. 2048: 45
GP9 No. 1200: 63
H-16-44 No. 1600: 89
H-16-44 No. 1601: 89
PA-1 No. 0771: 87
PA-1 No. 0781: 100
PA-1 No. 0783: 110
PA-1 No. 0785: 97
RDC No. 47: 122
RS-1 No. 0670: 97
RS-3 No. 539: 99
RS-11 No. 1409: 74
RS-11 No. 1411: 57
RS-11 No. 1412: 55
S-2 No. 0616: 59
Transfer No. 14 (tug): 23
0906: 51
0924: 112

Electric locomotives
EF-1 no. 088: 24
EF-3a No. 0155: 18
EF-3b No. 151: 43
EF-4 No. 300: 43
EP-1 No. 016: 31
EP-2 No. 311: 30
EP-2 No. 312: 34
EP-2 No. 325: 31
EP-3 No. 0351: 41
EP-4 No. 361: 19,
EP-5 No. 371: 20, 26
EP-5 No. 378: 48, 52
EP-5 No. 379: cover
Multiple Unit Cars: 19, 20, 21, 39, 44

Steam locomotives
0-8-0 No. 3605: 59
2-10-2 No. 3207: 60
2-10-2 No. 3217: 72
2-10-2 No. 3227: 73
2-10-2 No. 3228: 67
2-10-2 No. 3232: 68
2-10-2 No. 3235: 72
4-6-2 No. 1315: 117

4-6-2 No. 1335: 108
4-6-2 No. 1370: 91
4-6-2 No. 1375: 116
4-6-2 No. 1380: 107
4-6-2 No. 1387: 61
4-6-2 No. 1399: 114
4-6-4 No. 1402: 86, 119
4-6-4 No. 1405: 56
4-6-4 No. 1407: 82
4-8-2 No. 3311: 85
4-8-2 No. 3318: 88
4-8-2 No. 3323: 95
4-8-2 No. 3338: 60
4-8-2 No. 3343: 84
4-8-2 No. 3500: 66, 92

Passenger trains
Bay State: 86
Bostonian: 82
Cape Codder: 121
Colonial: 87, 96, 104
Day Cape Codder: 123
Gilt Edge: 97
The Hell Gate: 28
Merchants Limited: 52, 115
Morning Express: 100
Park Avenue Special: 91
Patriot: 36
William Penn: 26
Senator: 108, 109
Yankee Clipper: 110

Photographers
Abbey, Wallace W.: 52, 79, 80
Ahrens, John P.: 36, 39, 43, 69, 72, 73, 76, 82, 86, 91
Andrews, Scott: 104
Bennett, Jim: 31
Bowman, Fielding J.: 30
Brumbaugh, Wayne: 93, 95, 96, 113, 115
Cochrane, Kent: 21, 25, 37, 61, 66, 68, 71, 78, 84, 88, 117, 119
Collora, Gene: 74
Cudahy, B. J.: 122
Ditto, Pierre M.: 81
Dolkos, Paul J.: 19
Edgecomb, W. A. R.: 38, 93
Ellis, Wayne P.: 121
Fancher, W. A.: 100, 107
Gadziala, Gary: 26
Grabert, Charles H.: 51
Harvey, H. F.: 114
Hayden, Parker: 109
Ingram, R.: 123
Milner, Bob: 97
Meaker, E. R.: 51, 59, 60, 62, 90, 92
Meyer, Bruce: 28, 99
Netherbee, N.: 67
Obert, Charles: 42
Parker, C.: 110, 116
Phelan, Jim: 111
Plowden, David: 87
Pontin, H. W.: 56, 59
Schlegal, Frank W.: 17, 64
Screibman, Alan M.: 27
Shaughnessy, Jim: cover, 12, 32–34, 44, 48, 52, 53, 55, 57, 75, 77, 89, 112
Swanberg, J. W.: 44, 45, 70, 124
Tyrill, Alfred: 24
Wood, Don: 16